GERTRUD SCHRÖDER - LONG PING

FRIEDLICHER DRACHE

ENERGY OF THE FOUR ANIMALS

APPLIED QIGONG

THEORY AND PRACTICE OF QIGONG DANCING

Bibliographic information published by 'Die Deutsche Bibliothek': The German Library catalogs this publication in the German National Bibliography; detailed bibliographic information can be found on the Internet website: http://dnb.ddb.de.

1. Edition 2017

Publisher: Long Ping - Friedlicher Drache
Author: Gertrud Schröder Cover design: pepworx.de(sign)
Cover Picture: Jana Wippermann
Layout: pepworx.de(sign)

Production & Publisher:
BoD - Books on Demand, Norderstedt

ISBN: 9783746036847

Information & Contact:
www.friedlicherdrache.de | info@friedlicherdrache.de

CONTENTS

PREFACE

"LEARNING THE TRUTH WITH BODY AND MIND"
(Shinjin gakudo)
37th capture in Shobogenzo of Dogen

In Western philosophy and science from the antiquity until the end of the last millenium intellect and spirit have been placed at the forefront of thinking. Body awareness was not common, neither in theory nor in practice.

Then has been a change of paradigm in Western medicine and psychotherapy due to new perceptions in neurobiology and neuropsychology.

Human beings were considered more holistic. Body and mind were no longer separated. Body and mind no longer existed as counterparts and affect and cognition were no longer divided. The power of imagination and emotions influence physical processes and vice versa. Movement and postures have an effect on thinking and feeling.

In this context acceptance of traditional healing from the Far East is continually gaining ground. One aspect is the scientific knowledge, whilst the other aspect is fundamental experience.

Qigong enriches health treatment. It complements Western ways in viewing life in the context of thought and speech and by approaching life through Eastern meditation and body experience.

Gertrud Schröder's book is the essence of four decades of practicing Qigong, martial arts and Zen-meditation.

I met Gertrud in 2001 during a further education course called 'Affect Control Training' and I was immediately impressed by her physical presence.

As I studied medicine and psychotherapy I enhanced my knowledge. Analytic thinking and different theories and hypothesis were familiar to me. I had to understand that my intellectual knowledge of the relationship between body and mind were only the beginning, and I am grateful that Gertrud encouraged me during the following years to begin my own path.

She generously shared her profound knowledge with me.

Gertrud has an extraordinary personality. She is an authentic teacher always ready not only to teach, but also to learn. With an inexhaustable enthusiasm she developed her system with the four animal images and tested them in different areas.

The dragon is a mythical animal in Western and Eastern culture. Strength and ability are its attributes: in this sense long ping (peaceful dragon) is an exemplary mediator: she builds bridges between West and East extracting the best of both traditions for optimum application in current times.

In friendship

Brigitte Flegel
Psychiatric consultant and psychotherapist

PREFACE OF A SINOLOGIST

Interested in philosophy and the practical implementation it was only a question of time before we would meet in Freiburg. What I appreciate in Gertrud Schröder, also called Long Ping (peaceful dragon), is the dragon's mutual view of humans and the world: the character, flying in heaven, the dragon loves the vastness, the view and swimming, he values the closeness of encounter.

With an all-seeing eye she developed the inter- and transculture of her practice and theory. Animal exercises from the old Chinese tradition and Western teaching of the four elements were connected. Thereby she created her very own system called Qigong Dancing.

The system can be used in a lot of different fields in which human relationship plays an important role, for example, in kindergarten and schools as well as in social work and therapy.

This book describes the history of Qigong Dancing which is associated with Gertrud's biography. In the second stage she invites the reader to develop his or her own experiences and reflections about life which is even more attractive due to the practice of dance, power, mindfulness and concentration. There are body exercises to learn, but also descriptions of the experiences from her students. In their examples of use you see the full potential of daily life support and therapy. In this context you hear about „Affect control training" which means it is important to be aware of your own feelings in order to handle your own emotions and affects in relation to other people. Both are exercised and embodied: an intuition for the atmosphere of situations and connection to people, as well as the ability to act and react throughout your daily life.

I hope Gertrud's book will reach many people. People who aspire to a more collective, peaceful, aware and playful life all rolled into one. So they may acquire their own experiences as well as those with others in the expression of different aspects: the serenity of the bear, the grace of the crane, the energy of the tiger and the transformation ability of the snake.

Gudula Linck
em. Prof. for Sinologie, University Kiel

BRIEF INTRODUCTION

Experience and discovery, learning and development through motion has been the basis of shaping my life. I would like to invite you to a journey of discovery. We are on a journey and the image of the bear, the crane, the tiger and the snake are our companions. New paths will be opened through the medium of motion. New impulses will be engaged for more indepth observation and to become perceptible to change. It will grow into an opportunity for implemention in your daily life.

Together with Thomas Brendel, the founder of 'Affect Control Training' I developed a training which serves the inner and outer orientation of the world. In the meantime it has been adopted for practice in many fields, including institutions for child and youth welfare, crisis intervention, rehabilitation, psychiatry, corrections facilities, probationary services, psychotherapy, adult education, kindergarten, schools and special needs schools.

The four images of the animals are the gate to essential life themes. They provide supporting impulses for individual inner development. It is the basis for awakening curiosity and questioning.

The following questions are designed to encourage 'movement':
How do I represent my point of view? (bear)
What are my goals? (crane)
How do I commit myself? (tiger)
When and how do I adapt myself? (snake)

Gertrud Schröder, November 2017

BEAR

Inner attentiveness

Strength and serenity

To care about yourself

Grounding

CRANE

Grace and beauty

Clarity and vision

Having a goal

Openness to connect

TIGER

Acting with precision

Ready to fight

Resolution and energy

Decisive actions

SNAKE

Smooth moves

Adaption and transformation

Connecting opposites

Ready for a change

BEGINNING AND DEVELOPMENT
MY BACKGROUND

More than 40 years ago I began a quest for new paths, different ways of life and to find myself. It was high time for a new beginning , to abandon everything that was familiar to me and to seek a more enhanced consciousness. The driving power was curiosity. I was attracted to Berlin in search of freedom and independence. But I also experienced the abyss of a big city.

At that time I met Steve who later became my husband. After a time traveling together with a group of musicians we found new orientation and settled in Freiburg.

In practicing Zen-meditation, I learned a new perspective on life. New doors opened one after the other, a direct take on life, to live for the moment. At 22 years old, I had my very first touching experiences with Zen.

I continued my journey throughout the inner and outer world. It was at this time that I became fascinated by martial arts and started practicing karate. Discipline, structure and fixed procedures were part of the training. This was quite new to me, because until then I had refused inflicted structures from others.

Throughout the following years I worked in different occupational areas, studied and learned. At the age of 30 I started doing karate again. After some time of practicing karate I learned about Kung Fu at an advanced training course. I met a Kung Fu teacher. This was the beginning of 8 years of learning Kung Fu, Taijiquan and Qigong, and an extremely important period of my life. These years proved to be a transition from apprentice to journeyman for me. That meant daily practice, learning discipline and stamina.

Month by month I learned from my teacher, either traveling to his place or inviting him to run seminars in my hometown of Freiburg. I met people who I trained with during his absence. I organized seminars in Italy and France. After three years of practicing martial arts I established my own institute.

When I rediscovered Zen meditation, I started to practice Zazen, simply sitting in silence with my students, in addition to the martial arts. Early in the morning we practiced for one hour, just sitting and opening ourselves to silence and presence, the so-called Shikantaza.

During a Zen initiation I received my name „Peaceful Dragon" at the Zen monastery „La Gendronniere" in France . I am still devoted to this place, and a tradition of regular seminars have now taken place every year at Easter since 1989. It became a period where we practiced martial arts in the spirit of Zen. Once in a while musicians were invited and the first connections between dance, martial arts and music were born.

KARATE MEANT FOR GICHIN FUNASKOSHI (1868 - 1957)

- Teaching Karate Do (path) with Kata (patterns)
- No competition
- The spiritual aspect is at the forefront
- Does not initiate an attack
- Intuition is more important than technique
- "Don't think about winning, just concentrate on how not to lose!"

The images and associations of the animals in Qigong and martial arts became my training focus.

The practice center (dojo) in Freiburg was then established. Training for me was teaching four or five classes every day. The next step was to find larger premises, so I moved to my institute in the 'Fabrik für Handwerk, Kultur & Ökologie e.V' (Factory of Crafting and Culture). I decided to go public with my work and organized a conference for ´martial arts, meditation and healing´ in Freiburg. This was quite new at that time.

Teachers and masters from fields as varied as Qigong, acupuncture, Taekwondo and Zen presented their ideas. They shared their knowledge in workshops and panel discussions.

After the conference I treated myself to a martial arts course by the Chinese master Janet Gee in San Francisco (Cal.,USA). As well as enjoying a wonderful exchange of thoughts beween us, I learned to apply Kung Fu elements in spontaneous, free movements. This was an important impulse for the development of Qigong Dancing. In the following years I travelled to San Francisco several times and invited her to teach at my dojo. More education followed. For several years Qigong Yangchen (Qigong for cherishing life) became an important part of it.

In China on an international Wushu congress I became acquainted with a Shaolin monk whom I invited to Germany. He brought

me some paintings and calligraphies of the four animals of Master Ma. They immediately turn every room into a dojo.

My dojo grew. Health insurances requested me to provide prevention projects. I was asked to do seminars all over Germany. An article in a women's magazine spread the word of Qigong Dancing.

I continued to develop the concept of the four animal images. A teaching DVD of Qigong Dancing (2002 Warner Visions Germany) was produced. I declined the advice of offering the concept in gyms, but I decided to introduce my work to different social fields.

So Qigong Dancing was developed on my basic experience with Zen, Kung Fu, Taiji and Qigong including the animal plays of Qigong Yangshen and dance.

Consequently, the four animals bear, crane, tiger and snake replaced the five traditional Chinese animal styles of bear, deer, monkey, crane and tiger, as the former are far more associated with Western elements.

Another important pillar of my life became „Affect control training", developed by Thomas Brendel in 1989 to treat convicts who were selected for forensic psychiatry. He expressed the slogan „What is helpful for my clients can not be bad for me." In other words, the therapist must be self-aware and scrutinize himself in order to help others.

Over approximately two decades we ran about 30 advanced training courses for people in different fields of work and life and organized 17 expert conferences all over the country at different facilities. In doing so we acquired outstanding consultants from philosophy, education, therapy and politics for the idea of Affect control training.

Through eventful times the Dojo in my hometown of Freiburg was and always will be the base for my work as well as my sanctuary. A variety of experiences can be encountered within a safe space. An atmosphere of trust is essential for involvement in internal processes. The system of the four animal images is the basis for me, it is a universal principle of life.

The principles of the four animals are also the basis for my own teaching. As a trainer I have to represent stability: The virtue of the bear. Space is open for participants to feel safe.

For the quality of the bear his 'thick fur': I am able to handle projections, feelings and transmissions in a constructive way.

AFFEKTKONTROLLTRAINING A.K.T®

To move is a basic desire for a human being. It is resource, method and goal. Body and movement are the mirror and the key to handling conflicts. A central element in dealing with oneself and personal surroundings is emotional competence. Within the connection between the moving arts of the Far East and the systemic world view it is possible to explore communication structure and dynamics. They can be used for motion analogies. Terms like self-assertion can be experienced with a curious mind. With self-reflection there is an ideal opportunity for successful communication.

One of the fundamental ideas is the recognition that communication can be successful if there is a possibility of constructive reaction. The main focus is the best possible compromise for a manageable future situation.

Affect control training, which is orientated on move and reflection, is a learning curve for confrontation with the individual attitude.

In association with the crane as a trainer I need an overview of situations as I accompany the participants on their path to enhance their views and behavior.

With the energy of the tiger as a trainer I need to react fast in unpredictable situations. I convey precision, action, speech and expression.

With the agile snake I connect my ability to react in accordance with the individual situation of the participant.

Practicing ZEN meditation teaches awareness of the moment, beyond ready-made concepts. This intuitive 'being' penetrates all other areas.

My training methods have been further developed with the diversity of requirements. There are classes for kids, adolescents and adults as well as for individuals in conflict situations. Selfdefense, Zen mediation, for individuals in conflict situations. Self-defense, Zen meditation, martial arts, Qigong Dancing, assertiveness for individuals with or without handicaps, involvment in educational and therapeutical projects, but also the traditional exercises of Kung Fu and Taijiquan. Another aspect of my work in Freiburg is to offer institutional presentations and school projects; further education events over the course of a year, weekend seminars with guest speakers on specific topics, as well as performances by members of the Dojo are included.

It is the variety of impulses that has kept my work so exciting and fresh for over 30 years.

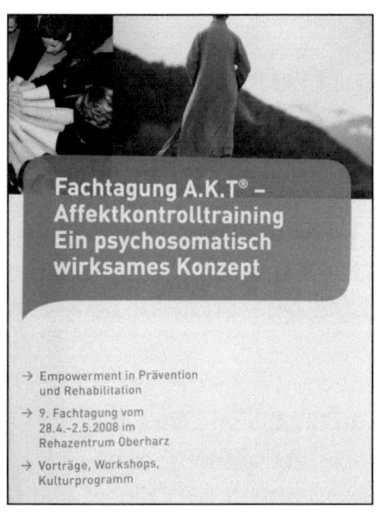

ROOTS OF QIGONG

A tremendous amount of research regarding the origin and development of Qigong can be achieved in bibliographies. Begin your search! It is an adventurous journey to Chinese philosophy and moving arts.

Qigong is described as to care for the energy of life. Different philosophical flows and the spirit of the respective era developed a lot of different systems of exercising.

In the 1950's a collective name for forms of exercise devoted to 'caring for life' was defined. It was called Qigong.

Throughout the 2nd century of our calendar another variation of caring for life energy emerged. It was developed by the Chinese doctor Hua Tuo as a therapeutic concept, called 'the play of the five animals' (WuQinXi).

Associated with the conversion phase of traditional Chinese medicine, this includes movements of the deer (wood), monkey (fire), bear (earth) and tiger (water).

They were later associated with the internal organs, energy spots and meridians. The idea was to create a flow of Qi throughout the entire body. Regular practice opens the perception for body and mood.

The connection to the animals and the conversion phase may differ, depending on the perspective of the masters of the system.
All these exercises are an expression and a practice of Chinese philosophy. The most significant aspect is the philosophy of Yin and Yang and the philosophy of Taoism.

The success is a balanced interaction between the energies of life. Yin and Yang describe the perspective of 'as-well-as' which underlies the knowledge that the 'one' only exists because of the 'other'. In other words, there is a choice. The spiritual space can be extended.

Taoism is the pursuit of life in harmony with nature. For the old wise men of China this was a way to explain the world with 'DAO', beyond time and space, beyond existence and nonexistence.

The wise man is acting by 'not doing' (Wu-Wei). That does not mean no activity, but appropriate actions at the right moment. Things are developing by themselves when the moment is right. In Taoism spirituality is explained in a simple and direct way. It is not promised faithfully, but connected to daily activities.

At a time no later than when Buddhism was gaining ground in China, Yoga was influencing life care. This happened directly after the time of Christ.

Buddhism refers to the tenet of Siddharta Gautama (560-480 AC), who called himself 'The Awakend One' after his enlightenment. In order to redeem onseself from suffering, Buddha teaches the 'Four noble truths and the eightfold path'.

LIFE IS SUFFERING
Bonding and attachment leads to suffering if our desires are not satisfied. Due to our desires, to maintain our comfort and to avoid unpleasantness, we try to control our surroundings in order that we may view our attitude towards life as acceptable.

SUFFERING HAS A SOURCE
Our reality is created by subjective experience. We create spatial awareness if we relieve ourselves of our concepts and perceptions.

THERE IS AN END OF SUFFERING
Comprehension of reality is to understand our illusions and to comprehend that the way to liberation is achieved through awareness.

THERE IS A WAY
The fourth noble truth is the eightfold path. The eight aspects of Buddha's teaching relate to each other by being practiced at the same time. These are Right View, Right Thought, Right Speech, Right Action, Right Livelihood, Right Effort, Right Mindfulness and Right Concentration. A successful synthesis born of philosophical Taoism and Indian Buddhism became ZEN (Chan, Chinese). Bodhidharma, who supposedly taught martial arts to Shaolin monks was the named creator of this synthesis.

Buddha accomplished enlightenment through the posture of seated meditation (Zazen, Jap.), during which the spirit is relieved of all judgemental thinking and no benefits are sought (Mushotoku, Jap.). The spirit is becoming clear, everything is being perceived, nothing is retained.

The thoughts flow like water. Walking Buddha's path, the individual nature can be recognized and inner peace can be found. Harmonizing heaven and earth and connecting them means letting thoughts and emotions pass by, calming the spirit and not holding on to anything. Our action and the action of others meet in response.

In ZEN, but also in martial arts, posture, breathing and concentrati- on are the basic practices. All attitudes of life are becoming ZEN. Getting intimate with one's self, and learning about one's true nature is the core of seated meditation (Zazen).

It is the condition of calm and stability, of alignment and composure.

THE CONCEPT OF QIGONG DANCING

After many years of experience with martial arts and working on Eastern philosophy, I decided to remember the roots of European culture. I started looking for images which are familiar to people who were socialized by Western culture. So I decided to combine the concept of the four animal images with the four Western elements of earth, air, fire and water.

The bear, crane, tiger and snake are particularly suited to this notion. They immediately conjour up spiritual images and open up floods of associations.

The bear, seen as a stuffed animal, triggers childhood memories. The term 'bears cave' opens the mind to perceptions of security, but also a fear of restricted space. The bear represents the desire for tranquility through his retreat into hibernation.

Due to his appearance, the crane represents grace and elegance. Living together in herds, but exclusion is also part of his image.
The crane's instinct for curiosity reflects departure and the discovery of new areas.

The tiger represents vitality and powerful performance. Associations with vigor, but also destruction are part of his image. The tiger's assertiveness is broight to bear in every challenging situation.

The snake is smooth and adaptive, but she also triggers a fear of the unpredictable.

In Christian culture she symbolizes the temptress to sin. In contrast, however, she is also used as a talisman in many other cultures. In China the snake represents the little dragon, who resides in heaven

(Yang) but also on earth (Ying) or in water, respectively, connecting opposites.

These four animals are the basis for Qigong Dancing, bringing awareness to the interplay between posture and mental-spiritual feeling. Predetermined forms of Qigong are the starting points for practice. They offer structure, stability and safety. This stimulates peace and concentration for the essence. As the form then progresses into free movements, the practitioner will experience an individual expression which will then be mirrored later in the form again. The exercises facilitate continuous development of the movement with the inner self and others with analogies relating to everyday life, thus providing a 'practical Qigong'. This can then be implemented in everyday routines.

The arc of suspense between inner and outer world, between you and me, between individuals and groups, being alone or in company offers a variety of different approaches which will be integrated in the process. Every student has the opportunity to involve his individual character into Qigong Dancing and to develop his own personality. The practitioner decides how far he can go without feeling insecure. Thus, it is the path to independent self-help.

The protected space of the dojo provides an optimum precondition for engaging in a deeper understanding.

THE FOUR ELEMENTS

Replacement of the Chinese five changing phase system was an important step in my posture training. The conversion phases illustrate the changes of the five material conditions of wood, fire, earth, metal and water. The system of the four elements is familiar to Western tradition. That is the main difference to Qigong styles taught in the Western world. An important step in developing my posture training was to replace the Chinese orientated system of five transformation phases with the Western system of the four elements. It is common in Western tradition, thus, a significant difference to the variety of Qigong styles taught in the Western world.

Even in the ancient world, the four elements of earth, air, fire and water has been considered the primary substance of physical being. The recognised founder of the four element tenet was Empedocles (483-423 BC), a greek philosopher and physician. Platon (427-347 BC) and Aristotle (384-322 BC) continued it's development and turned it into a system. Aristotle added the ether to the system, because he took it for a basic quintessence. Magical ideas were even interwoven in the system by Paracelsus (1493-1541 AC) and other contemporary alchemists. A Western antique typology developed from this concept is still valid today. According to this typology, earth represents the melancholic, air represents the sanguine , fire represents the choleric and water represents the phlegmatic.

In the artistic symbolism and in daily life, the four elements are still present. Knowledge of the four elements can be identified as Mem, representing a cultural pattern that is passed on by way of images, speech, symbols and traditions and underlies permanent change. The analogy of the four elements and the four animals is easy to follow. The method of Qigong Dancing allows a connection between those two concepts.

FOUR ELEMENT SYSTEM

SENSORIMOTORIC LEVEL	SPIRITUEL LEVEL	COGNITIVE LEVEL	EMOTIONAL LEVEL
BEAR	CRANE	TIGER	SNAKE
EARTH	AIR	FIRE	WATER
EXPERIENCING THE WORLD	DISCOVERING THE WORLD	WINNING THE WORLD	EMBRACING THE WORLD
STABILITY	OVERVIEW	ASSERTIVENESS	INTEGRATION
CALM	GRACE	WILDNESS	LOVE
TRUST	EASINESS	ASSERTION	TRANSFORMATION
WARM-HEARTED	VIGILANT	FORTIFIED	FLEXIBLE
INDIVIDUAL ASSOCIATIONS	INDIVIDUAL ASSOCIATIONS	INDIVIDUAL ASSOCIATIONS	INDIVIDUAL ASSOCIATIONS

This chart illustrates assignment of the four levels of communication in context to the four animals - sensorimotor, spirituality, cognition and emotion. The four elements and the different associations complete the chart. The chart can be extended by individual ascriptions. A separate consideration will be helpful in order to understand the interaction within the whole picture.

In the four element system of Qigong Dancing, we assume that every experience and encounter happens on the four levels of communication. They are all related. The principle of self-similarity corresponds to the different levels. Our mental awareness programs generally activated by life-experience are stimulated by movements with and without partners, perceived conceptions and music, then summarised in words and implemented in personal relations. A learning process is generated in movement. Awareness of fractal logical interrelations and the translation of experiences from one level to another broadens perceptions.

The insight that communication always occurs on these four levels allows messages to be discerned and brought into context. Knowing your own biography facilitates the ability for successful communication. All four levels are simultaneously effective in each individual animal image.

The sturdy posture of the bear, for example, conveys access to the knowledge of individual strength. On a spiritual level, he is reminded of traditional rituals of connectivity. Exploring individual history and searching for personal resources necessitates a cognitive level. At the same time, images of the bear elicit sentiments on an emotional level, such as a yearning for security.

熊

書於一九九九年

四月

中國 山東省

濟南市 時辛

七十五歲 逸叟

馬文寬

The bear represents stability and connection with earth.

SENSORIMOTOR
Communication with our body by posture, facial expression, gesture and speech melody is described as sensorimotoric level.

Sensorimotoric level: **THE BEAR**

- SELF-AWARENESS
- PHYSICAL RESOURCES
- STRUCTURES
- SELF EXPRESSION

Air, expanse and effortlessness are attributed to the crane

SPIRITUALITY

The spiritual level, our understanding of comprehensive coherence of life expressions in everything that we think, feel or do.

Spiritual level: **THE CRANE**

- MEANING
- VISIONS
- CONTEMPLATION
- TRANSZENDENCE

書於
一九九九年
四月
中國山東省
濟南市
七十五歲
逸叟
馬文寬

Fire, dynamic and vitality is the energy of the tiger

COGNITION
Processing of knowledge happens on a cognitive level. This involves logical thinking, the ability to abstract and expressing experiences with words.

Cognitive level: **THE TIGER**

- WILL
- ASSERTIVENESS
- VIGOR
- DETERMINATION

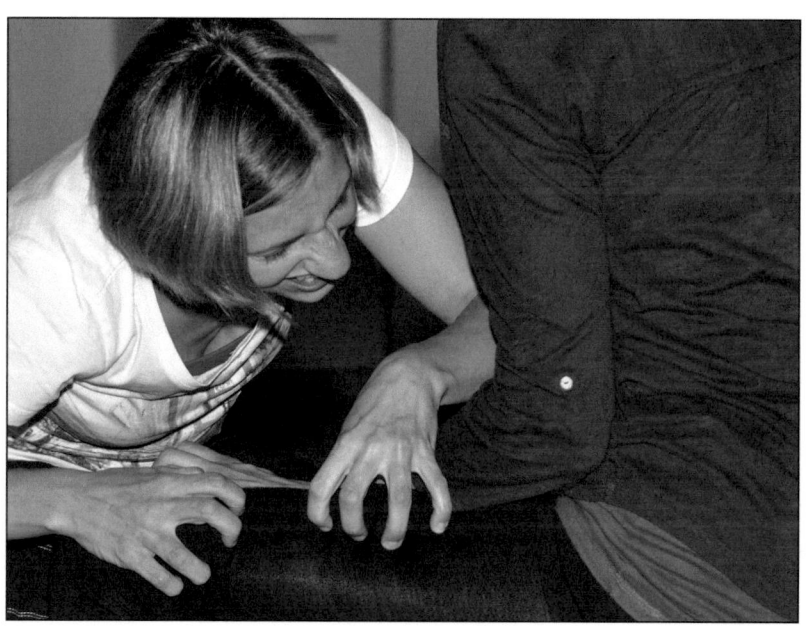

中國 山東省
濟南市
逸叟
七十五歲
馬文寬

一九九九年
四月
書於

The snake is allocated to water
She is flexible and adaptive

EMOTION

The emotional level colours our thinking, feeling and acting. Emotions express our feelings and behavior. We are touched by the impulses from the inner and outer world.

Emotional level: **THE SNAKE**

- ADAPTION
- SENSUALITY
- ENJOYMENT OF LIFE
- METAMORPHOSIS

In Qigong Dancing a new way is presented:

The traditional exercises of Qigong are being enhanced by free, individual moves, elements of dance and martial arts. The internal shape can be expressed by the body.

The effects of postures taken deliberately to the internal shape can be controlled.

Habits can be changed by exercises. As we admit to process of exercise we determine the quality of experience.

In order to reflect the experiences the approach of physiotherapy and the theory of resource-based solution-orientated attitudes have been integrated.

Qigong Dancing connects Eastern and Western knowledge and wisdom.

The exercises are a posture training for the everyday life and serve as a support to health maintenance and the desire for individual expression and development.

THE DANCE WITH THE ENERGY OF LIFE

Dancing is a healing ritual. It is located in our experiences and it has always been part of our religious and cultural life. Motion is like a language in development.

The styles of dance are changing. They are socially accepted or they break standards. They may even lead to changes. Dance expresses the zeitgeist and can touch deeply. It triggers emotional conditions and supports a feeling of togetherness. Emotions are becoming clear. There is a frame and open space to express them.

Dance is an expression of your personality. It opens ways to develop creative potential and to discover individual choices.

Qigong Dancing integrates experiences by repeated motion patterns and individual moves. Free dancing occurs from deep inside. Spontaneous impulses develop by the theme which is offered by the trainer.

Interrelations of behavior and motion can be recognized by interacting with members of the group and can be changed by experimenting with different images. First a ground has to be created. The next step is to 're'discover your own visions, to transfer them into action and link them to your experiences. The dispute with individual issues will be put in the foreground.

The expression of a particular emotion becomes easier by the experience of the animal metaphors. Initially, it is the bear that strikes, the crane balancing on one foot, the tiger that shows his teeth and the snake that touches. We can use the 'power of the animals' to become conscious of the reasons for our individual behavior.

Actual issues of life will emerge. The body as an access gate to the soul can very fast make hidden potential and the inner suppression visible. We may encounter 'forbidden' and 'forgotten' topics.

The image of the crane, for example, can provide the experience of grace and ease, but also that of confinement.

Associated emotions like the fear to express oneself and to be open towards the beauty of life can show abysses of ones soul.

Qigong Dancing teaches how to integrate these 'forgotten' parts. Prerequisite is the guidance to become aware of the individual body posture. Music supports the motions and helps to be put in different moods.

There is room for playful but also combative aspects. Motion enhances cognitive and emotional learning. It opens the door for growth and maturation.

The variety of experiences in Qigong Dancing helps to take responsibility for constructive as well as destructive parts of the individual personality. Thus you gain internal and external space to feel free. The processes of healing and reconciliation will be put in place.

THE FOUR ANIMALS
AND THEIR ASSOCIATIONS

People of all cultures have imitated the skills and qualities of certain animals to get connected with their power. Native people always had their sacred totem and power animals. In fairy tales and narratives, basic human characteristics are connected to animal images.

The four animal images that are being used in Qigong Dancing present basic qualities: grounding, erection, presence and mobility.

Additionally there will be presented different themes of other fields of knowledge that fit to the specific quality of the animal images. The model of this basic life issues is of common validity.

In order to classify it, I would like to focus on different mindsets.

THE BEAR

The bear symbolizes the connection to the earth. Through the bear grounding, stability, calmness and relaxation will be experienced. We can trust the earth and draw sufficient strength of it.

Physical exercises with the image of the bear strengthen the individual inner center as well as moving and acting from it. We learn to stand on the ground and be capable to stabilize.

A feeling of security to be happy in your own skin are good keepers in times of crisis.

The bear symbolizes power. He is thick-skinned and hard to influence. If necessary he just takes what he needs.

Humans and the bear have a special relationship.

Even 30 thousand years old paintings at the cave of Chauvet in Ardeche (France) show this connection that was probably practised in rituals.

Bear cults and myths are to be found in many different cultures. For example, in Greek culture the bear was connected to Artemis, the goddess of hunting but also connected to other divinities.

In animistic beliefs like in the tradition of the Ainu people or the natives of Hokkaido in Japan, the worship of the bear plays an essential role, according to the written record.

By the image of the bear, eather by observations or by adopted ideas, a diversity of themes occurs, that can be tackled.

QUESTIONS CONCERNING THE BEAR

· How do I care for myself?
· Who or what is stabilizing myself?
· Where do I find my cave?
· Where do I find security?
· In what I can trust?
· What does grounding mean to me?

ARCHETYPICAL

The bear is associated with the female archetype 'mother', the principle of nourishing and reliability. A common expression says 'to bear a child'. On the other hand the dark aspect is the dominating and abusive mother. The male principle is the 'king', the protector and preserver. The dark aspect is the tyrant. In ancient Greece the woman was the keeper of the house and stove and it was an honor to take this place. The dignitaries had their meeting place at the 'state stove'.

TECHNIQUES AND EXERCISES

In martial arts powerful and soft techniques can be associated with the bear. These are wrestling, boxing, as well as retreating and stabilizing.

A BEAR STORY
Noah, 11 years old

The little bear cubs played on the meadow. They rolled to the right and to the left. Suddenly they heard a deep rumbling noise.

The bear children winced and tried to hide themselves in the grass. But when they saw who it was, they immediately knew they had no chance to hide. It was a full-grown male bear. The cubs knew how dangerous full-grown bear males could be. Slowly they sneaked backwards into their cave. The bear came closer and closer.

Suddenly the cubs ran into their cave, closely followed by the male bear. One of his paws hits after the little ones and missed just close.

Finally the mother of the cubs returned from her search for food. When she realized what happened on the scene, she interfered immediately. She positioned herself on the hind legs, hitting the air several times.

The male bear jinked and attacked from the side, but the mother turned around hitting towards the male again.

Slowly the male bear moved backwards. But once more he attacked from the other side. Again the mother pushed him back. Now the bear actually gave way. He went two steps backwards, then jumped forwards, but then he definitely disappeared.

Again mother bear had proved her steadfastness.

ASSOCIATED THEMES

LEARNING THROUGH THE BODY

Life-experiences are positioned in our body. These are our habits and skills like cycling that we will never forget. The memo-
ry for space and time, also moods and encounters with people
are memorised in our body. The neuroscientist Antonio Damasio
shaped the expression 'somatic marker' physical signals that are
retained in our body and triggered by stimuli. These so called
somatic markers can be positive or negative. We can train our
perception of these stimuli to have more options to decide. For
example, when I have to wait too long for an appointment and I
decide to experience the upcoming emotions consciously and im-
partial, I am going to observe different body sensations. Instead
of perceiving discomfort or tension and anger I can put myself
into another state, into the image of being centered in myself
like a bear. I can make an independent decision instead of being
defined by the circumstances.

Body sensations constantly influence our mind. It depends on our mood what we prefer to perceive, how we are going to interpret it, how we are going to look at it, what we are going to keep in mind and what refers to former experiences. This is how we construct our individual logic.

The tools in Qigong Dancing are the body with its predetermined postures and moves, exercises with partners as well as group experiences.

After the exercise the experience in motion will be put in words, so it becomes conscious and comprehensible.

By creating analogies the specific patterns of feeling, thinking and behaviour become visible and changeable.

By transmitting them to the spiritual, cognitive and emotional level, confirmed patterns of behavior can be verified and taken off.

The first step is to be ready for critical self-reflection. This might cause awareness of patterns that are sensed as unpleasant. This has to be viewed in individual responsibility. The coach will draw attention to this side effect.

DEVELOPMENT OF HEALTH - SALUTOGENESIS

The salutogentic approach by Aaron Antonovsky, an American-Israeli medical sociologist, is an enhancement and amendment of the Western deductive research approach. That has dominated the Western worldview for centuries . The question 'why do humans get sick?' is extended by the question 'what makes humans healthy?'.

According to the Salutogenese model health is a process where different personalities have access on different resources. The focus will be set on abilities that help us to stay healthy or to become healthy respectively.

This is not a static condition but a repeated developing process. We need the trust that puts us in the position to solve difficult life issues. Antonovsky considers the stream of life as a river and explains this metaphor in his work:

People swim in river full of danger. A medicine orientated at deficits tries to save the drowning whereas salutogenetic thinking shows how to learn to swim.

In this model a central aspect is the sense of coherence, that means a feeling of meaningfulness, manageability, comprehensibility.

Therefore we can look for role models and learn from others who have mastered a crisis.

The significance we give to stress factors is essential too. The trust on solutions and the capability to recognize and to use the offered resources in order to stay healthy is a process that lasts a life time.

SELF - EMPOWERMENT
Self-empowerment means to be responsible for ones actions. Resources can be recognized and used. Problem-orientated thinking will be replaced by looking for solutions. Consequent rethinking is demanded. Therefore different options for action can be offered. To use them can be an important life-support.

THE CRANE

The crane symbolizes start and new beginning.

The flight of the crane opens 'New Horizons' and the overview makes it possible to find new perspectives. Its upright posture helps to focus on the essential. The exercises of the crane enhance our capability to develop visions, open up new spaces and stimulate the willingness to walk on new paths. Situations can be observed from a distance.

On one hand the crane has a graceful appearance in beauty and easiness. But on the other hand he is ready to strike out for a hard punch with his wing or stabbing with his beak.

QUESTIONS CONCERNING THE CRANE

- What exactly should be my goal?
- What do I want to change?
- Which risks appears by the overview?
- When do I need a sharp and when do I need a soft view?

WHAT CAN BE INTEGRATED IN DAILY LIFE

- Widening of the view and proactive thinking
- Vigilance and balance
- To start and to plan goals
- To change perspectives
- To experience own limits but also to set limits

ARCHETYPICAL

In female archetype we associate the healer, the wise woman, with the crane. In myths it is also the witch who looks in other worlds. Her power can be used for good or bad. The male equivalent is the sorcerer or the black magician.

TECHNIQUES AND EXERCISES
Powerful and soft methods from martial arts can be trained with the image of the crane. Wide and swinging movements with the arms create distance. Stick and knife methods stand for the sharp beak.

IMPULSES FOR INTROSPECTION

Graceful beauty – Clarity and vision – Eyes fixed firmly ahead.
The crane opens up and unfurls. With his wide wings he displays elegance and effortlessness. With the image of the crane, I countenance new impulses and embrace them as my own.

How should I envisage my road ahead? I set out, ready to explore new territory, assured in my quest and soar to acquire an encompassing overview. Setting myself boundaries allows me to mature, and feeds my curiosity for new accomplishments and foreign places, fully aware of the risks and obstacles which I may encounter along the way.

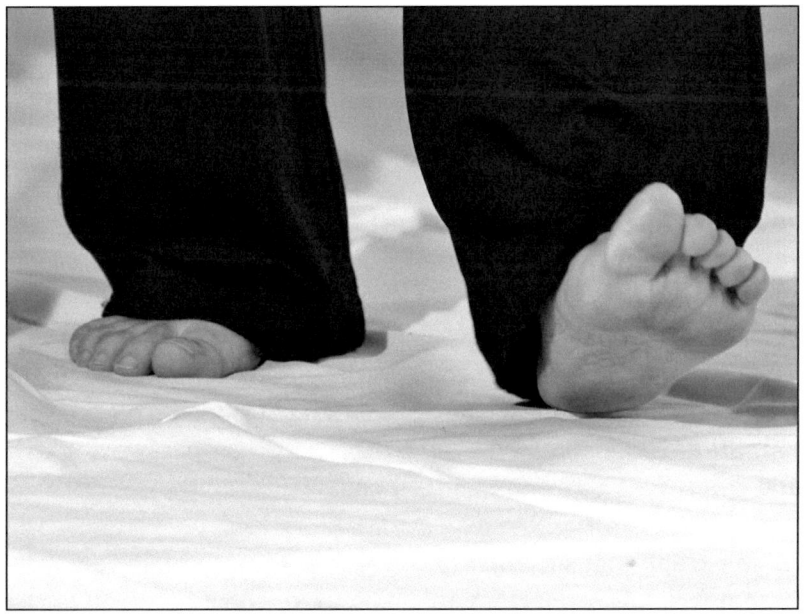

ASSOCIATED THEMES

COMMUNICATION

All living systems have similar basic structures and dynamics that are comparable. Luc Ciompi, a Swiss psychiatrist developed the idea of fractal affective logic by using the insight of chaos theory. This led to the theoretical basics of self-similarity of structures and processes. We use this knowledge in our work with the images of the four animals and adopt it to the creation of our daily life.

In the following this is going to be explained by an example of a group process out of a seminar.

Two groups are being formed while each group has to present an own mood.

One group picks up the quality of the 'bear' by using the voice in order to express strength. The other group going along with the quality of the 'crane' is acting in order to show open mindedness and curiosity.

After a while both groups become aware of each other. The group members go into motion patterns of archaic moves. One is stomping, the other is fluttering.

The dynamic of the group changes depending on how the members of the group tune in to the situation. Depending on the specific life experience and meaning that every member is giving to it the group dynamics and arrangements are changing.

In an exceptional situation like that it becomes visible very fastly that well known pattern are being used. The interaction of the group members correlates with their every day communication.

We express our attitude by our mood while our counterpart is going to respond with its individual mood. Due to the awareness of the own attitude alternatives can be found.

Try this experiment: Sit down for a minute with forward bent back, constricted shoulders, dropped corners of the mouth and watch your mood change. Thereafter keep sitting with your back straightened, corners of the mouth up and straight looking forward and watch the change of the mood is taking place.

THE MISSION 'ONE THOUSAND CRANES'

Thousand folded cranes are a lucky charm. Cranes are a symbol of hope and confidence. In Japan Origami cranes made of paper are being gathered and given away as a gift for special occasions.

Once I was teaching a class at a correctional facility in Austria that opened doors and created worldwide connections. One of the inmates, Peter, had folded a thousand cranes and sent it to me. We used them to create a Mandala and I decided to start a donation campaign.

At the following seminars and classes every participant got the opportunity to get one of these cranes in exchange of a donation. The entire money was sent to the Rescue Foundation in New Delhi, India. The Rescue Foundation organizes the liberation and rehabilitation of girls who where kidnapped and forced to prostitution.

Perpetrator/victim compensation happened although the involved did not even know each other. Traditions were linked to true life and the memes forwarded.

MEMETIC

Available information creates our reality and so do our experiences. We often define truth as what is acknowledged as true by the majority..Current life experience and moments connect with forwarded stories and history for generations. We are permanently influenced, gather information, aware or unaware, work on it, qualify them and respond to them.

Depending on its meaning a meme can be a chance or a risk. It can enhance or restrict our capabilities to act. If we know this we can decide how to handle it.

CLARITY BY ASKING

Do you still know? Or do you already ask?

These quotes were expressed by the already deceased master of RelösA (ressource solution approach) Berthold Lomberg in his seminars, in order to express an attitude that can be called the 'fostering of the curious beginner'.

The experience of a student tells descriptively that it is worth to take a closer look at an apparently chaotic structure that is then revealed to be a meaningful artwork by changing the perspective.Simultaneously it is a call to leave familiar paths and not to keep trusting the used preoccupied believes.

This attitude is also a call to leave deficit oriented thinking and to take a look 'over the rim', to find out what is possible.
Interest, curiosity, courage and enthusiasm are required.
It is helpful to express questions and to trigger thinking processes. Thinking processes provide new impulses.

The following questionnaire serves as an orientation in terms of individual goals. It serves as a support to move from desire to goal.

Scrutinizing every single step can make the way to the goal more manageable.

The criteria to name a well formulated goal comes from the resource and solution oriented concept of Steve de Shazer.

CRITERIA TO DEFINE A GOAL
– A WELL-ARTICULATED GOAL

The more precise a goal is defined, the better the results can be checked. The following 5 topics can be used as a manual:

1. Express in positive terms, no negation

2. Process oriented, single steps must be manageable

3. Here and now, the start must be clarified

4. Articulate as precise as possible

5. Self-controlled, the goal must be realistic

THE QUESTIONNAIRE - ASK BEFORE COMPLAIN

Check the difference between desire and goal

DESIRE:
GOAL:

Well-articulated goal:
(see criteria to formulate a goal)

- How exactly should it look like?
- What exactly do I want to achieve?
- What can I do for that?
- Who can support me?
- What do I need?
- What do I have (can) already?
- What should never happen?
- Which conditions must be complied for a start?
- What kind of commitments have to be made?
- What am I allowed, what am I not allowed to do?
- What am I going to do, if it does not work?

Answering these questions is helpful to get through various clarifying processes in order to formulate a goal. They are a support in therapeutic processes but also a help for self-help.

REASONABLE CORRELATIONS - COHERENCE

The sense of coherence consists of several components: I can understand the situation, clear solutions are visible, it makes sense to me to become active. If something is considered as reasonable, a room for action will be seen and the challenge can be accepted.

If I can handle the challenge, confidence will be developed and even straining circumstences or difficult phases of life can be handled. Experience helps to fend off stress and to take things in our own hands. If I see reasons, there is a basis to activate resources and to get engaged. This attitude leads to freedom of decision and individual responsibility. It is a support for crisis management and solution findings. We are not suppressed by fate, but have influence on the arrangement of our life.

Take time to think about your individual course. Start writing a diary by answering the following questions:

• Which values inspire you in your life?
• What is your orientation?
• Which purpose do you see in your life?
• What comes to your mind thinking about the virtues, associated to the four animals bear, crane, tiger and snake? Warm hearted, vigilant, defensive, mobile?

THE TIGER

Fire is the element of the tiger. The tiger represents presence and straight, precise action and self-confidence. He puersues his objectives with determination. Every single action is evident and straightforward.

Qualities we connect with the tiger are drive and courage to handle difficult life-situations. His dark sides are reckless behavior and the misuse of power. Destructive outbursts of fury complete the image.

QUESTIONS CONCERNING THE TIGER

- How can I resist?
- When do I show 'teeth and claws'?
- Am I ready to fight?
- How can I enforce myself?
- What is it worth fighting for?
- When is violence a solution ?

WHAT CAN BE INTEGRATED IN DAILY LIFE:

· Power, strength and courage
· Authority, strong appearance
· Vigor, determination
· Assertiveness, ability to handle conflicts
· Willingness to take a risk

ARCHETYPICAL

The tiger correlates with the female archetype of the Amazon. She represents the autonomous female force. The dark side, which is the destroyer, represents revenge and destruction.

The male archetype is the warrior who engages self-determined for an object. The mercenary does not care about cause and master.

METHODS AND EXERCISES:

Powerful methods from the martial arts teach to fight with 'teeth and claws' when it is needed, but also to act smoothly in lurking and silence.

A TIGER´S STORY
from Noah, 11 years old

The big tiger approached a deer. The moment it was about to jump, it saw two ravens watching the scene.

The tiger ignored them and jumped on the deer. When the deer realized that the tiger was following, it was too late. With a strong bite it was over. The tiger dragged its prey under a tree.

Just like vultures the ravens circled around the tiger and its prey and lowered some meters away. The ravens were not the only ones which were interested in the prey. A wolf appeared from one side, a bear appeared form the other side. Even a wolverine joined in.

The attackers came from all four directions. First the bear tried to reach out for the prey. Yet the tiger was obsessed to defend its prey, so the bear retreated. Motivated by the bear's action the other animals attacked, too. The tiger remained steady and ousted the animals one by one. But they tried over and over again.

When they realized that the tiger kept defending its prey, they retreated one after another. This turned out to be the hardest ordeal of life, but the tiger had mastered it with its persistence.

IMPULSES FOR INTROSPECTION:

Stealth in negotiation - Readiness to fight - Drive

The tiger asserts himself, he knows precisely the things which are worth fighting for and reacts quickly and precisely when it matters.
Qualities with which we associate the image of the tiger are of vigor and courage, of keeping his claws sharpened and seizing opportunity.
To dictate a very clear YES or NO and to be ready for action in the here and now. What is worth fighting for?

I value him being at my side, aware of his might, but also of his destructive power.

ASSOCIATED THEMES

RESILIENCE
Resilience means mental resistance. It is the ability to memorize your own strength in crisis situations. Some people become torn apart by internal conflicts and heavy blow. Some people can see stress as a challenge. We are not born with these qualities, but we have to learn them by developing a healthy feeling of self-value. With these qualities unforeseeable difficulties and serious illnesses can be managed better.

INTELLECTUAL SELF-DEFENSE
Intellectual self-defence needs proven methods and solution strategies. Practical solutions for daily life in professional and private life are part of it. The goal is cooperative communication, clearity in word and action as well as avoiding manipulation. We have to respect other people´s boundaries.

Analogies of intellectual self-defence in martial arts and their proven applications with all resulting consequences need be be praticed. In work and daily life situations it has to be tested and explored.

Martial arts and emancipation, learning to fall without a downfall, self-assertion and self-support are the learning goals.

NAIKAN

Naikan means introspection, to look inside yourself. It is a method, which was originally developed for prisoners in Japan. Meanwhile Naikan is practiced in many countries not only in prison, but also in Naikan-centers, where people stay for one week to practice this way of self-observation. The challenge is to observe and clear the own life story being supported by a Naikan teacher during this process. In guided stages the participant can decides the depth of this introspection.

"We barely have time to pause anymore, to stop our lives and see ourselves. We are always busy, without knowing why we were born, where we came from, or where we are going. We do not have time to think about our destination, and most of the time we do not even notice that we cannot know it. Is your life also too busy for you to notice that there is a beautiful flower on the path?" writes Prof. Akira Ichii in his book "The Essence of Naikan".

The three central questions in Naikan are:

- What has a person done for me?
- What have I done for this person?
- What difficulties have I caused?

For many years Naikan has been part of my own practice and it also became part of my teaching. It is a valuable opportunity to solve conflicts. Those who have no time for a Naikan week, may instead engage themselves with this questions on a regular basis.

THE SNAKE

The snake is a symbol of change. The coalescence of opposites, 'the cycle of becoming and passing', will be experienced immediately.

Characteristics like mobility and adaptability are associated with the snake. She assimilates to her surroundings, so she can survive in changing conditions. Her smoothness will be learned by motions.

The ability of shedding means inner and outer development, renewal and rebirth.

In the eastern mythologies, the snake symbolizes development and adaptability. In Christian symbolism the snake is associated with falseness and insidiousness. Fears to be crushed and strangled can be triggered by the image of the snake.

QUESTIONS CONCERNING THE SNAKE:

- Am I smooth?
- Am I flexible?
- Am I ready to adapt?
- How can I protect myself when I am sensitive and vulnerable?
- To whose tune do I dance to?
- What does sensuality and acting with relish mean to me?

WHAT CAN BE INTEGRATED IN DAILY LIFE:

- Smoothness
- Unconditionality
- Release the old and welcome the new
- Joie de vivre (joy of life)
- Temptation and seduction

ARCHETYPICAL

With the snake we associate the archetype of the temptress. In Greek mythology the Hoares, the mistresses of the hours, danced every night for one hour celebrating their service of love.

They also were guardians of time and guarded the gates to heaven. The Hetaera, the companions in ancient Greece, enjoyed a great social prestige. These women were highly educated. It is said that the Hetaera Aspasia, who lived in the 5. century B.C., interfered with Sokrates and helped him with his speeches. Even today in Japan geishas enjoy a high social prestige. The dark aspect would be the prostitute, where the body is considered as a merchandize.

The archetyp of the lover stands for the adoration of a woman while the pimp sells her like goods.

METHODS AND EXERCISES

Martial arts techniques practiced with the image of the snake are powerful entangling and crushing, but there is also smooth retreat and release.

IMPULSES FOR INTROSPECTION:

Lithe movement - Adaption and transformation - Connecting opposites

The snake symbolizes readiness for change, to let go of the old and to prepare for new ways. Danger and testing situations, painful shedding and mastering life in a new skin are both fate and opportunity for the nature of the snake. What ballast would I like to jettison? Flexibility of body and soul allows me to smoothly traverse the irregularities of life and to overcome sharp edges with versatility. Am I flexible? Can I adapt to new situations?

The joy of sensuous feeling and doing frees me from upset and other bothersome complexities, although I accept the hazardous maelstrom of unrestrained vicissitude.

ASSOCIATED THEMES

HOW TO HANDLE CONTRADICTIONS

Often we are confronted with contradictions which are hard to endure. People with less tolerance of ambiguity feel stressed very quickly by those situations and try to recreate their familiar situation without reflection. It is important to develop tolerance for versatile andcontradictory situations which cannot necessarily be solved, but have to be accepted. The attitude of 'as well as' instead of black and white thinking promotes balance.

The Qigong exercise 'connect heaven and earth' conveys the contradictions of stress situations. The somatic exercises and the training of a consequent 'resource and solution oriented approach' creates new options to act with the objective to master difficult situations in life and to gain power for the professional and personal everyday life.

DIALECTIC

The principle of a dialectic view is another entry to a deeper practice and is considered as a bridge to Ying/Yang, the principle of the ancient Chinese view of the world. Dialectics allows the 'as well as', leaving the dualistic 'either/or' behind.

In contrast to pure dualistic thinking which is constituted in 'either/or', not knowing the 'as well as' and therefore going into passivity. The key word in dualistic thinking is 'and'.

So there is not only 'black and white', but an infinite variety of 'shades of grey'. The recognition and comprehension of different views allows a variety of decisions.

THE BOTTOM LINE (QUINTESSENCE)

In quintessence the essential, the main thing, is being expressed. In Latin it is originally the 5. element, called ether by Aristoteles, the Greek philosopher. In India ether is the center of high energy and the space that contains everything. In ancient China this was turned into the all-embracing concept of vitality Qi.

The quintessence of Qigong Dancing is the connection of the basic qualities of the four animals. Thereby we associate some fundamental issues out of a stream of archetypal images.

Archetypes (C.G.Jung) are images, retained in collective and individual mind, that are based on existential human experiences like birth, death, heath, and disease.

Archetypes (C.G. Jung) are images stored in the collective unconscious mind. They are based on existential human experiences like birth, death, health, and disease. They also represent desires, phantasies, fears and coping strategies. The concept of the archetype has its lingual background in Greece and means origin and pattern (archè), model and antetype. (typos).

The images are as old as human social systems and take effect in all humans. They are based on the experiences and traditions of our ancestors and connected to our own imaginations. To the opinion of C.G. Jung similar symbols and images exist in the traditions of all cultures. Therefore he derived the thesis that all humans carry primordial patterns which lead back to the genesis of mankind.

Basically an archetype is neither positive nor negative. It reveals that all patterns of human behaviorcan be used for a better life.

In the four element system the basic archetypes are connected to the four animals.

ANIMAL	BEAR	CRANE	TIGER	SNAKE
MALE ARCHETYPE	KING TYRANT	MAGICIAN CHARLATAN	WARRIOR MERCENARY	LOVER PIMP
FEMALE ARCHE-TYPE	MOTHER „MOTHER HEN"	HEALER BLACK MAGICIAN	AMAZON DESTROYER	SEDUCTRESS HOOKER

These archetype patterns are waiting to be kept in balance and be realized in the individual personality.

Our personal images to these associations are filled with our experiences, memories and prejudices, that can be seen in a new way.

The symbol 'connecting heaven and earth', stretching the arms upwards and firmly standing on the ground, can be found in cave drawings and rock engravings of early civilizations. This archetypal human image 'back then and today' holds a fundamental importance for coping with everyday life. Timeless integration of all aspects can be experienced.

The exercise 'connecting heaven and earth' in all its portability symbolizes the basic human need of safety and security as well as of development and maturity. The balance between those energies is task and goal in every moment of our life. This means to take responsibility for our attitudes and actions. At the same time the four animals will attend us with their qualities associated with the four levels of communication.

Being in resonance with it means concentrating on the essentials of life, namely to keep the tension between reality and vision elastic for life-friendliness.

ABOUT MUSIC WITH THE FOUR ANIMAL IMAGES

The following text was written by Christoph Schwarz, a musician and trainer from Vienna. He has been attending my seminars with his live music for many years. Our intense collaboration creates dense moments for everyone involved, as the atmosphere is directly translated into music:

I became acquainted with the 'power of the four animals' in the course of my training as an affect-control trainer. Examining the various qualities of the animal images awakened my musical interest in finding different sound qualities for them and creating sounds to accompany the physical motions.

Music and sound emanate from the moves of the player and of the instruments' bodies. They occur in an in-between space, fill and transcend the boundaries between the inside and the outside. Sounds create atmospheres and shape transitions. They have been used since time immemorial to mediate between the inside and the outside, the individual and the group, between humans and deities, between heaven and earth. Similar to body language and verbal language, sound transports messages and creates connections. Sounds create spaces and can change the quality of an atmosphere in internal and external places.

Music and sounds are ephemeral and always provisional. They are not here to stay and quickly fade away. But they can reverberate and deepen their impact with motion. Using music as a support and as an 'amplifier' for moving experience processes such as working with the 'power of the four animals' is therefore an obvious choice. The musician has to translate the many aspects of the individual animal representations and their analogies into sound and create the space in which the participants' individual experiential

journey can take its course. The goal is creating sound passages for potential movement paths and reacting to spontaneous events. Another important aspect is enabling transitions between different poles (e.g. steadfast and light, far-sighted and precise, defensive and sensual).

BEAR – THE SONG OF THE EARTH

Pulse and rhythm structure and determine human existence. In addition to other chronobiological processes, the heartbeat and the breathing rhythm shape our well-being and our health. A clear and straight rhythm creates a good basis. Warm sounds, predominantly in a low frequency range, convey tranquility and safety, from which power and strength can develop.

The pounding of the bear's steps on the ground, the scraping of shaggy hair against the tree bark, the puffing in the bear's den, the awakening of the playful bear cubs, the roaring of the feral giant rearing up: the female bear's rhythm is the rhythm of Mother Earth. She slips into the den to reemerge in the spring, like the humming of the midges dashing by, the fragrances of herbs drifting by, the musician's sounds building up in the room and disappearing again, all the while conveying support, safety and protection.

CRANE – THE SOUND OF THE AIR

Like melodies moving over the musical scale, the crane is on its way. The play with pitch, the covering of distances in tonal leaps and the melody's dynamics combine with energetic, sometimes uneven rhythms. As the perspective changes, the harmonies change as well. The whirring overtones of the voice express aspects of vastness, departure and clarity.

The crane player is sitting up straight and purses his lips. With the power of the Earth, he makes the guitar strings resonate, lets rhythm flow into the room, and the voice takes off into the air. He oversees the room with mellow eyes, absorbs the physical agitations and plays them back. Chords which emanate sweetness and confidence carry away the flock and smoothly transition into jagged rhythmic accents in which boundaries are explored and fought out. Heavenly visions can fall to the ground like feathers, so that goals become clear and the first step goes into the right direction. The first note determines the entire piece.

TIGER - THE POWER OF FIRE

The vigor and potency of the tiger are reflected in the dynamic of the rhythm in powerful warrior chords and crystal clear musical actions.

As a tiger the musician is lurking in his corner. Then, nimbly and quietly, he sneaks across the drumhead. As the beats become fuller, the paws nestle against the ground, the grass is pushed apart with constant breaths, and the hands are waiting for the right moment to attack. The ground trembles with the drum roll, a roar speeds through the air. The tension erupts in a powerful cry, a short and eerie silence marks a stop and prepares the next move.

SNAKE - THE MUSIC OF THE WATER

The snake player feels the solemnity of the occasion. His hands move up and down the violin's fingerboard with abandon, just like the snake creature slithering through the sand and gliding across the water. In glissando and trill the sounds conflate into a flexible being. Sounds and atmospheres are wandering around. The last sound has to depart in order for the next one to arrive. The violin's melody circles around recurring themes, the snake takes hold of its tail and forms the circle of wholeness. It thus unites sound and silence, rhythm and arhythmicity, harmony and dissonance, high and low, sound and noise in the perpetual murmur of aliveness and transience.

The snake player feels the solemnity of the occasion. His hands move up and down the violin's fingerboard with abandon, just like the snake creature slithering through the sand and gliding across the water. In glissando and trill the sounds conflate into a flexible being. Sounds and atmospheres are wandering around. The last sound has to depart in order for the next one to arrive. The violin's melody circles around recurring themes, the snake takes hold of its tail and forms the circle of wholeness. It thus unites sound and silence, rhythm and arhythmicity, harmony and dissonance, high and low, sound and noise in the perpetual murmur of aliveness and transience.

Music is like everyday life. If I feel what I am playing and thus allow others to share the feeling, encounters can succeed. If the course participants can be with themselves, they can surpass themselves. Translating moods into sounds, absorbing the atmosphere of the moment, like a brush dipping into the paint pot and applying sounds to the canvas. Coloring the room in such a way that moods can unfold and people in their motions are allowed to develop an impact together. This is accomplished when the music refers to the moment and to the others, when a dialogue between the musician and those who are in motion can unfold. The musician's presence and the sound protect direct and open up, allowing everyone to venture into the emerging in-between spaces, at the right distance, and out again. Between Me and You, Outside and Inside, Wish and Reality, Vision and Goal, Heaven and Earth: Music expands its sail there.

'The sounds reach me and set my body in motion. The music inspires my moves and carries me through the room. Powerful and strong. The expression and the movements of my body in turn inspire the rhythms and sounds and change the music. Giving and taking. Dynamic and aliveness. Leading and following, in an interactive exchange which is hardly noticeable from the outside'.

(Excerpts from an experience report by Christoph Schalk)

BASIC EXERCISES OF THE FOUR ANIMALS
ATTUNING EXERCISES

'Opening the joints'

- Shoulder-width stance.
- Turn your head to the left and to the right, eyes following the move.
- Move your head up and down, eyes following the move.
- Twist your shoulders.
- Extend one arm to the front.The move will be carried out by twisting the elbow. First, the palm is being directed ahead, than back to the body.
- Extend both arms to the front, alternating, bend the wrists and swipe down the palms.
- Starting with the thumb stretch every single finger between index and middle finger.
- Rotate spine from the right to the left, beginning at the tailbone. Arms follow easy.
- Rotate pelvis.
- Put one foot easyly forward on the ball and rotate knee.
- Lift knee and rotate foot.
- Pinch the ground with both feet and release grip.

QIGONG EXERCISE
OPENING THE JOINTS
YouTube (Video)

105

'Connecting heaven and earth'

- Keep feet in parallel, hold hands with palms up in front of the lower abdomen, fingertips directed towards each other.
- Move arms up, turn palms out when reaching chest level. Move them over your head to the side of the body.
- Now, palms are turned to the right and left. Breathe slow and steady.
- Make a receiving, scooping semicircle move and breathe.
- Hold the breath, turn hands, palms down, and move them downwards in font of the body. Bend body down by sagging move of the arm. Exhale at the end of the move.
- During inhaling make a receiving, scooping semicircle with your hands and lift them in front of your body.

QIGONG EXERCISE
CONNECTING HEAVEN AND EARTH
YouTube (Video)

BEAR EXERCISES

Basic stance: mudra of the bear

- Starting position: keep feet in parallel.
- Hold hands in easy fists in front of the abdomen, smoothly closed around the center of the palms. At this position of ease, think of the center of your stomach, feel it and breathe steadily.
- Activate the arches of the feet.
- Lower the body's center of gravity, activate the abdominal muscles.

Bear exercise: the fists of the bear

- Starting position: mudra of the bear.
- Draw a semicircle from the outer to the inner until chin level is reached. Open fist and wander palm down the centerline towards abdomen.
- Practice both sides alternating.
- During lifting the arm the shoulder blades stay in position.

QIGONG EXERCISE
BEAR
YouTube (Video)

CRANE EXERCISES

Basic stance: mudra of the crane

- Starting position: keep feet in parallel position, slightly turned outwards.
- Erect backbone, crest seem to be „opened" towards heaven.
- Arms bow on either side, elbows pointing down, fingers are slightly stretched, palms are opened forwards.

Crane exercise: the crane is spreading his wings

- Starting position: keep feet in parallel, cross hands in front of abdomen.
- Put weight on right foot, settle left foot easy in front. Put weight to the front foot, the rear one is set on the ball without carrying weight.
- The sides of the little fingers open the move downwards and to either side, moving the arms in a wide bow in front of the fore-head on eye level. Index finger and thumb show a triangle.
- Palms show ahead and are being kept at this position.
- Arms sink slowly while weight is being put on the rear foot. Left foot in front will be pulled back.

QIGONG EXERCISE
CRANE
YouTube (Video)

TIGER EXERCISES

Basic stance: mudra of the tiger

- Starting position: horse stance, center of gravity lowered
- The back is straight
- Arms are bowed in front. Hands are being set down in front of the abdomen and form a tiger's paw.
- The gaze is set straight forward.

Tiger exercise: the tiger shows his power

- Starting position: shoulder width stance.
- The hands form „tiger paws" in front of the lower abdomen.
- Lift „tiger paws" to the center of the breastbone and lead palms in front of the breastbone to the forehead in a soft bow.
- Strain hands and release.
- Twist body to the left, set down left foot with pressure, knees slightly bent (weight distribution 60% in front, 40% in the rear, this may differ).
- Hands, palms down, are being formed to claws (grasping prey).
- Pull back front foot in basic position, arms are being pulled back in semicircle bow to starting position. Start with right side.

QIGONG EXERCISE
TIGER
YouTube (Video)

SNAKE EXERCISES

Basic stance: mudra of the snake

- Starting position: Keep feet close together.
- The body is straightened.
- Palms are put together in front of the breastbone.

Snake exercise: the hands of the snake

- Starting position: Keep feet close together.
- Palms are put together in front of the breastbone, fingertips show upwards.
- Starting at the pelvis, the body moves in wavelike to the right and to the left. The hands move in counter rotating waves, led by the fingertips. The head stays in firm position.
- The lower hand holds the upper hand.
- All joints are in motion.

QIGONG EXERCISE
SNAKE
YouTube (Video)

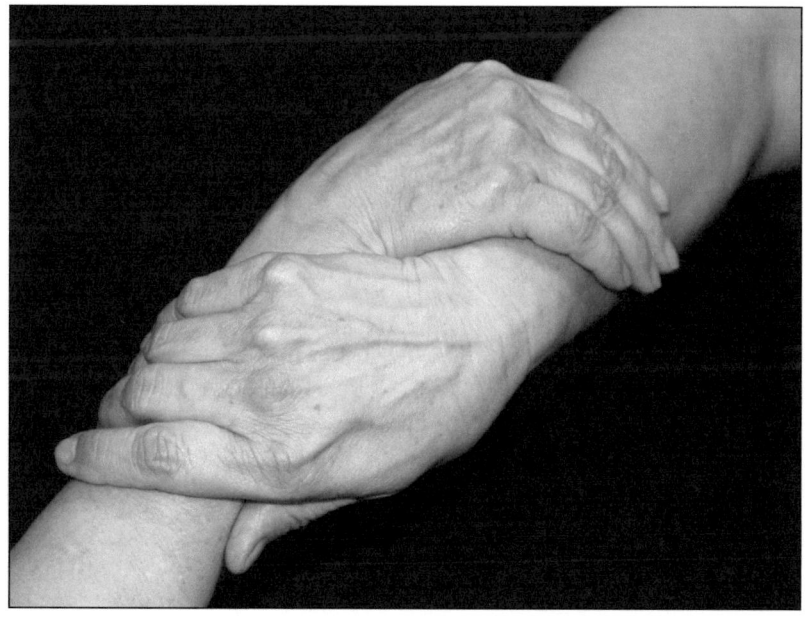

EXAMPLES OF USE
PREPARING CHILDREN FOR LIFE

Especially for children it makes sense to integrate moving in classes. Therefore, Qigong Dancing offers teaching concepts, that are already being used in practice. Prerequisite is further training for trainers and a crucial view on structures of the daily routines at school. At this point working with parents will be proving as useful.

Experiencing - Discovering - Learning – Developing by moving with the four animal images

The conceptual background is based on the 'four phases' that are orientated at the following themes and questions:

1. Stabilisation: self-care, self-confidence, self-regulation, tranquility and strength
Questions: What keeps me firm? How do I care for myself?
Further themes: rules and framework, firmness, affects, attitude

2. Orientation: perspectives, goal setting , setting limits, communication skills
Questions: What do I want to learn? How do I limit myself?
Further themes: visions and goals, separation, communication, and cooperation

3. Assertion: Action planning and application, courage
Questions: How do I assert myself? What am I fighting for?
Further themes: conflict-solving, strategies for enforcement

4. Integration: Adaption, mobility, pleasure
Questions: Am I ready to adapt myself? How can I protect myself? What do I want to change?

In the foreground of motion orientated training stands the individual self-development by playing and elements of martial arts.

Besides the motor and physical abilities

- Problem-solving
- Interpersonal
- communicative
- emotional
- responsible

behavior is being taught together with the necessary skills. Throughout the training there is space to gather experience and knowledge to develop the competences above.

It is useful to put these themes in regular classes and to engross it by homework.

Concerns and goals:

- support of the personality
- strengthening of self-confidence
- improving and developing the perception of the body
- motor development
- concentration
- respectful interaction
- nonviolent management of conflicts
- discovering own skills
- developing individual strengths
- social structures, linking with others
- experiencing limits and extending them
- well defined rules for fighting
- practicing flexibility and coordination

Usually children love the animal images and they prepare their own texts and present them on a martial arts performance.

Paula, 10 years old
The bear represents the element earth and has a firm stance. Appearing clumsy at first sight he holds strength and power. The bear has a very strong self-confidence. He always knows what he wants. In Kung Fu, the moves of the bear were adapted from his natural way of living.

Mia, 10 years old
The crane – firm and free. The moves of the crane are full of easiness. The crane stands on only one foot with a great sense of balance. The exercises of the crane are being used to find tranquility. By the use of defensive moves, similar to the crane, we keep distance from the opponent.

Finn, 11 years old
The tiger can clench really fast, but he also can retrieve his paws into the former position. In Kung Fu he is also a mediator. He is strong, but only attacks if necessary. The element fire fits to his powerful moves. In Kung Fu there is a lot to learn from the tiger.

Liam, 10 years old

The snake represents the element water. She moves fast, smooth and agile if there are new paths to discover. In dangerous situations the snake gives ways but stays always calm. Her moves are steady like waves on the water. She is strong but also reluctant. She thinking only for herself and does only what she considers right.

The 'Play of the Four Animals' touches different levels. The children train their perceptive faculties both internally and externally, as well as their ability to move, coordinate and socially interact. The exercises are based on the 'virtues' of the four animal pictures, and the children playfully deal with basic life themes in order to strengthen themselves for life. You experience, discover, learn and develop skills for shaping your life through movement.

ASSERTIVENESS TRAINING FOR CHILDREN AND ADULTS

MARIO MAYR AND THOMAS RINNER

Assertiveness training is a holistic way of learning. Required competences that will be needed to handle conflicts are being developed and strengthened. The 'power of the four animals' provide new 'self-conscious' strategies that will be learned playfully and are being adapted to the daily routines.

Each animal holds individual focuses that offers valuable impulses for a variety of different situations. First of all the term violence has to be defined: Violence is always a solution of choice when throughout an actual situation no other option is available. This has to be checked and acknowledged in order to develop alternatives of action and to get out of an 'attitude of powerlessness'.

The transfer to the four levels of communication does always work – physically, doctrines concerned , verbally and emotionally. Assertiveness, prevention, self-defense, and de-escalation are in focus and will be integrated in the training.

Exercises:
• Performance, perpetrators look for victims not for opponents
• Classification, show boundaries
• Ability for self-defense
• De-escalation

Holistic approach:
• Sensimotor level – learn to handle the condition of the body
• Spiritual level – check individual doctrines
• Cognitive level – courage to face difficult situations
• Emotional level - deal with deep feelings

SUGGESTIONS CONCERNING THE FOUR ANIMALS

Assertiveness - Bear
Stability, Body posture

- Technique: punch
- Power training

Strengthen body and mind to master steadfastly difficult situations.

Prevention – Crane
Set boundaries, View to evaluate situations properl

• Technique: karate chops
• Learn to fall down

Use the momentum to stand up if you have been falling down. Thats useful for surprising attacts on all levels.

Self-defense – Tiger
Show self-confidence, Act in the right moment

• Technique: powerful grabbing
• Fitness training

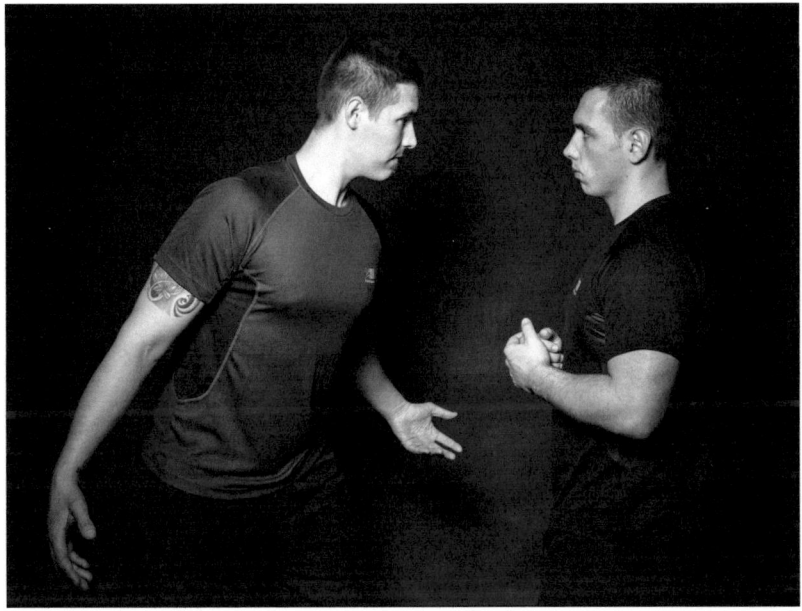

Learn to fight to avoid to fight.
Those who don´t fight have already lost.

De-escalation – Snake
Flexibility, Find surprising strategies

- Technique: lever
- Mobility training

Fast reactions are possible by the interaction of smoothness and power.

Our philosophy:

THE QUALITY OF ALL FOUR ANIMALS IS NEEDED FOR APPROPRIATE REACTION.

FIELD RECORDS

PATRICK FROTTIER
WORKING WITH ANIMAL IMAGES

As a psychiatrist, specialized in forensic psychiatry and child-psychiatry and having worked with mentally disordered offenders and aggressive children for most of my career, I have experienced different approaches to understand and treat people, whose ability and motivation to change their behaviour is seriously limited or wanting.

Quite often the classical therapeutic approach is based on language which is asking, listening and responding. It is a talking cure. And more often than wished for, this approach is not successful, as talking in these cases is not the way of communication these people are used to. To react is not to talk but to do something, to hit, to run or to ignore, to fight, to flight or freeze.

What can we do if the talking cure is not possible anymore?
One option is working with images instead of words, working with your body instead of your thoughts, working with emotions instead of your intellect.

Since 2004 I have been trained to use images, emotions and the body as tools by Gertrud Schröder and Thomas Brendel, who are the two founders of Affect-Control-Training, to make the difficult task of changing aggressive behaviour happen. They taught me that body posture, inner values and emotions are cohering with each other. Changing the posture will change your emotions and on the long run your inner values. Body, soul and mind are an interacting unity, so that changing one of these three artificially separated units will include a change in the other units. So instead of words we have a set of images that are associated to body postures and to emotions. The images are furthermore symbolizing the basic needs, which have to be satisfied to enhance personal development and growth.

As images the founders of this special way of treating personality traits and behaviour choose four animal-images: the bear, the crane, the tiger and the snake.

THE BEAR

The bear stands for my personal integrity: 'who am I, where do I stay, what do I stay for?' The bear represents the need for the provision of inner and outer stability: the physiological needs as all the basic issues of survival and security. In the representation of the body it is visible in the stability of one's body posture and in the representation of his mind it is observable in the way one is defending his opinions and values. The emotion of defending oneself is anger, as anger is felt whenever somebody is trespassing my limits. Expressing anger is therefore a way of restoring my personal limits. And it means resisting contempt as an unsuccessful und unfavourable way to re-establish the weakened self-value whenever it has been hurt.

THE CRANE

The crane is a symbol for the intended movement, the first step in a direction: "where do I want to go, what is my goal, what do I want to achieve?" The crane represents the need for self-actualization, the readiness to challenge oneself, to leave the safe ground and to explore the world. The representation in the body is the way we move and react, supple or stiff, fast or slow, light or cumbersome. In the representation of the mind it is observable as the skill to observe attentively without being judgemental, to anticipate what is going to happen and to make plans to realize what you whish for. The emotions of exploring the world are surprise and fear: the willingness to be surprised expands the need to explore, fear limits this need. Fear signals possible danger. Whenever the danger is real, the fear is adequate and a way to protect myself has to be found. Whenever the fear is independent of any danger, the origin of the fear has to be explored. Otherwise every development is hampered through my fears.

THE TIGER
The tiger is the symbol for effectiveness, action and goal-oriented behaviour: 'what is my duty? and: what is to be done has to be done now'? The tiger represents the need for self-actualization and for achievement. It is therefore connected to the need of self-esteem. Positive self-image and self-respect, recognition and respect from others are the issues of the tiger-imago. The representation of the body is visible in the physical fitness, strength and training-state of the person. The representation of the mind is observable in the discipline within the every day life, how structured a conflict is managed, in the capacity of analysing a problem. Joy is the emotion of self-actualization and achievement, sorrow the emotion of loss and fail. To accept loss and defeat as necessity of life, to mourn for some time and to continue the work, that has to be done, with joy and courage, this is the tiger-mentality.

THE SNAKE
The snake is the symbol of integration and mutuality: "how am I connected to the world, how does the world reflect on me? How do I evolve from the "I" to a "we" and "us"? What does it mean to love or to be loved?" The snake represents the need for "belongingness", for social acceptance, friendship, love and corporate identity. The representation of the body is visible in one's agility and ductility. The representation of the mind is observable in the capacity to adapt oneself to various settings and situations, to integrate adverse opinions or viewpoints, to accept ambiguity as a basic fact of life. The emotions of belongingness are interest and

acceptance and in its strongest mark is love. To share your interest, to be interested in others, to be mutually committed in every aspect of the world is the aim of the snake.

For more than 12 years I have been working in numerous and different settings with the concept of the four animal-images that has been created by Gertrud Schröder. It has been a highly successful approach to treating people, who are sometimes supposed to be untreatable. And it has been a continuous path of learning and personal growth for myself. I am very grateful that I had the opportunity to become a part of the four-animals family.

WOLFGANG GRATZ
PENEL SYSTEM AND THE FOUR ANIMAL IMAGES

Correctional institutions are particularly social places. Their very function impresses clear distinctions (inside - outside, guard - guarded, protector of law - lawbreaker). This in turn tends to lead to negative stereotypes between staff and inmates.A harsh tone is prevalent in everyday conversation. Studies have shown a background noise of verbal aggression in general communication, not alltogether isolated forms of violence amongst the inmates, but also between inmates and staff, with the legally legitimized use of violence by prison guards at the forefront.

If one were to take the stance in the conventional atmosphere of a seminar, that public servants are not necessarily all well-meaning, and that prison inmates also have their good sides, that the compliance with standards is also not always maintained by law-abiding citizens, the discussion becomes a little more difficult and will rarely result in a winning side.

From my own personal experience, I believe that the particular strength of affect-control-training (German A.K.T®)is adopting different perceptions and behavior patterns toward defensive attitudes. A.K.T® stimulates debate with personal and social underlying structures at a non-verbal existential level.

With the physical exercises reflecting the four animal images in particular, and discussion of corporeal experiences gained as a result, the participants may find dismay within themselves. This does not only convey the everyday mix of good and evil, but also the synchronicity of strengths and weaknesses.

These are core topics in the penal system. People can be approached in this manner which is just not achievable on a verbal level.

A.K.T® was gradually integrated into the Austrian penal system over several years initially as part of advanced training, and then in the education of law enforcement officers. As a result of various personnel changes, however, also due to the fact that the climate within the Austrian penal system has not necessarily changed for the better, A.K.T® is currently only being applied in niche areas.

Positive experiences have nevertheless been documented in this regard. It was shown, that some of the participants understood the conveyed message: you must learn to deal with your own destructiveness, you must work on it and you have to accept that the perpetrator also has his positive attributes. The other participants could not accept this. In any case, affect-control-training with its four animal images is clearly more suited to personal learning and reflection processes, as well as to changing or refining professional attitudes, more so than conventional adult educational theories.

To be more specific:
The image of the bear appeals to the Austrian prison guards, and it is even stipulated in the Austrian Penal Code (§ 22) to treat all detainees „calmly, sternly and firmly". This is also part of the job description. That considered, we can identify with the bear as an animal which cares both for itself and for others and creates an atmosphere of security.

The daily routines in a penal system essentially revolve around monotony, which can very easily lead to personal demoralization and a decline in personal abilities. The main aim is then just to get through one day after the other with as little commotion or exertion as possible.

The image of the crane represents upheaval, and a new beginning. We encourage the formulization of personal goals and to implement at least minor changes to daily routines. This could mean for example, taking a different view of detainees or treating them with more respect, or even an improved personal distinction of forms of destructiveness encountered in everyday life. Vigilance does not necessarily mean mistrustful limitation, it can be also be a form of open mindedness and provide a general overview. It is possible to disassociate oneself from the severity of the prison institution, at least intermittently, and to establish a boundary, a sense of ease and mobility from an outside position.

The defensive abilities of the tiger were well received by the prison guards, however, it was not so easy to convey to them that violence, whilst a solution, should be a very last resort. To implement this through the effectiveness of personal relationships, the power of words, to reach inside others because it is coming from within them, proved an interesting topic, and because one can permit themselves not to implement this, but rather to administer it to others, as long as this does not have a damaging affect on their environment and does not cause one any difficulties.

A typical working day within a penal institute revolves heavily around dichotomy: to assert oneself, to expect others to conform versus smooth introduction of oneself in the institution, intensive group pressure, how he sees himself as a uniformed monitoring body, yielding, even adapting himself and thus relenting a little.

The image of the snake provokes debates concerning different forms of balance in the adaptation of oneself and of others, however, also about which forms of joy and fun can be recognized and made more likely at work.

The episode character of A.K.T® with its four animal images as a contribution to the training and advanced training of prison guards can be explained with practical procedures, personal changes and specific decisions. It may also be perceived that a difference has been made which was too great for the penal system, not only because this system is moving in an opposite direction, namely towards rigidity and an increase in negative stereotypes, as well as developing stronger distinctions.

What remains, however, are personal changes and further developments which were influenced by the four animal images in a number of people. As I know from various personal contacts, numerous people are much more conscious of their professional roles, are more aware, and as a result are just a little bit more humane. There are also those who implement what they have learned and experienced in their work with inmates and other people.

The four animal images can be removed from educational schedules and curricula, but never from inside the people which they have reached, touched and moved.

PHILIPP PÜMPEL
POSTURE TRAINING

II am not fascinated by a technique, but a posture which is expressed by word, gestures, thoughts and actions.

For me posture is like 'to provide of my disappointments and hopes, my fears and troubles but also my beautiful experiences'. I am available as the person I am, and not the person I want to be - my person in its whole area of tension, in theological words 'mysterium tremendum et faszinosum'. How does this posture change within me and the interaction with my environment? I am not the 'advisor' anymore 'the professional social worker' (which I am not anyway) or 'goal-oriented employee '.

I am human and I make myself available as a human being, my 'being part of the world' and this way the world closes in, too. I am no longer the closed off professional, resting in myself.

How can I make this individual available during a training session? In my opinion a capability and a given fact is required. I am going to start with the capability: the so called 'curious beginners mind'. It is the ability we can learn from children, who are sedulous touching and imitating everything, asking questions and admire the world with wide and curious eyes.

The given fact that we need is a 'safe space', a 'dojo' where no 'right' way exists, but where each and every individual can test their own ways. It should be a place where everybody has the opportunity to 'be how he is and to become who he is not yet' as V. Frankl said, who described the human as an optional being, that always has new choices and never is caught in a fixed state of being.

All of a sudden it is possible, that 'clients' become 'persons '. There is no given program, which every client must do and which automatically leads to the desired goal. Instead there are as many programs as there are people in the 'safe space'. Now, encounters occur while everybody learns from each other, defining the frame where common ways of solutions will be found. Encounters that are not characterized as 'teacher-student situations' and that are not lead by 'right and wrong' categories. It is no longer the 'consultant' who meets the 'client' but the 'Me' meets the 'You', which V. Frankl described as 'the I is becoming the I by the you'.

How can this encounter take place? We meet in this safe space, the 'dojo' and by practicing the four animal exercises together we get into an exchange. Every participant will be capable to slip into the 'You' with his 'Me', the 'You' of the bear, the crane, the tiger and the snake.

Saved by the different images of the animals, incredible learning spaces will be opened for the 'Me': there is room to develop the loving side of the bear as well as the belligerent side of the tiger.

THOMAS FROM VIENNA
AN ALTERNATIVE CONFLICT SOLUTION

Some time ago I was invited to a party, because I had been released from prison after a term with my custodian was finished. I was there with a good friend of mine. The party was in a typical Vienna tavern. There was a lot of alcohol and one moment after another the situation escalated. One of the guests started to insult and threaten all attendees..

At some time he walked towards me. All of a sudden I felt the 'bear' in me, I straightened up, my breath was deep and calm. He started insulting me and I got him involved in a discussion. Eventually, he stressed that he was not afraid of me. I answered in a very calm way that there is no need for being afraid of me. He should calm down and so he did.

This was the first time I felt what this posture training ment and what it means to use it in daily life. In this situation I felt the stability and calm of the bear. Just to feel its presence was calming. I also understood the crane, because it was very important for me to keep the overview in this situation to see the other guests in the tavern and to calm the aggressive ones. I felt the presence of the tiger in this situation, not to hide myself. The quality of the snake showed up at the end when I invited the young man for a beer and the situation finally became relaxed.

CARSTEN SCHUBERT
MIND-BODY THERAPEUTIC ASPECTS

Nearly twenty years ago I met Gertrud and Thomas for the first time 'Affektkontrolltraining®'- seminar. From the following inspiring examination of their highly esteemable work and actions, a meaningful and stable connection developed for me and my work, which is still active today.

Especially the participation in Gertrud's courses and offers helped me in the following years to gain profound and formative insights and experiences around the phenomena warm-heartedness, alertness, resistance and agility. These have their fixed and recurring place not only in my physical therapy work with the multi-dependent young people who come to our clinic for treatment. Most of them have also been damaged by severely hurtful experiences that directly interact with the addiction.

Of course most patients in my clinical context are initially difficult to get them interested in the physical aspects of their existence. After all it was precisely the unsatisfactory and barely bearable physical conditions that led to consumption and addictive behavior and thus to the effective refusal of the conscious own BEING and the perception of what IS.

 It is also challenging to find a fit between the previous life worlds of the patients and the 'therapeutically initiated counter worlds', which are now to be mediated in a new way and which strive for a sensitive ability to be present. New experiences of support and attitude need to be stimulated. And if this is to be done in parts also via the path of confrontation with Bear, Crane, Tiger and Snake, a convincing mediation and communication effort between the contradictory worlds mentioned above is required.

This is all the more likely to succeed if the basic therapeutic approach is a creative and comprehensible one and, in addition, is supported by a radical acceptance of the solutions presented by patients - however absurd they may seem to us at first glance. This creates the necessary confidence over time to accept the invitations to experiment together and to approach one's own body perception carefully.

Qigong Dancing has the advantage that the name already refers to a connection to western culture and thus stands in the way of a premature assignment to a purely eastern martial arts tradition with the correspondingly strict regulations and special strangeness. This often makes it easier for patients to find a suitable approach to the new levels of experience between 'heaven and earth'and the four animals.

The process of softening and letting go of the patient's usual and safety-giving ways of seeing, experiencing and dealing with oneself and others is usually exciting but arduous. It is characterized by many more or less hidden resistances (cheeky smiles, devaluation of the offers internal shutdown and over-gaining provocative refusal, and much more) accompanied. However most of the time I succeed in convincingly conveying the meaningfulness of the new experience with a view to the chances of becoming healthy, at least on the cognitive level. The accompanying movement work can set important supporting anchoring and change impulses due to the limited time available. However these have a lasting effect on the continuous development of bear, crane, tiger and snake virtues, if patients want to and can take them with them into their everyday life by means of continued practice.

On the movement experience level it is possible to focus on both general and specific developmental topics related to the dependency disorder. For example, the 'heaven and earth' combine the aspect of balance and equilibrium on the various levels, while at other times the stability or the more or less fluid mobility felt as a prerequisite for an adaptable self-reference and also to each other. Finding your own centre without distraction - being a central element of coexistence experience can be seen and developed in all Qigong Dancing exercises as well as the aspects of experiencing breathing.

For example, the sky and earth-movement sequence intensively activates the lower, middle and upper respiratory tracts and can be clearly felt in their respective vitality.

The attention to the breathing process accompanying the movements can also lead to a rhythmic basic pattern that is formed early in the body. Their recovery is usually accompanied by considerable calming and stabilization.

Comfort-to-be-able, the organization of sufficient stability and steadfastness (it is easy to overthrow) as well as the ability to delimit the experience of coexistence, which often corresponds with the permission to be allowed to do this without sanctions are recurrently central building sites in the wake of addiction.

At least just as important is the attention to earth as an imaginary seat of one's own resources and competences and to heaven as the epitome of the directions and goals that want to be pursued and achieved by making use of them.

Neither is easy for many addicted people as they often had to gain mastery in self devaluation, negative self-image and low self-confidence in order to practice their use of addictive substances in then chosen uninhibitedness. This includes, as it were, hiding the future-oriented consequences of one's own actions and euphemistically embellishing them in a trivialising and unrealistic manner.

How why with what consequences are the predefined motion elements of the bear, crane, tiger and snake archetypes executed? Am I experiencing the movements as beneficial, caring for me? Is it possible to develop a basic attitude towards others characterized by respect and warm-heartedness, especially when practicing partner-related? How can we achieve a secure hold and a sufficiently good bond that should be satisfied, taking into account the two central basic needs for continuous self-development and reliable dissolution and connection?

These are some of the selected questions that accompany the practice units and can stimulate the joint search for satisfactory answers. Answers found are then again experienced, tested and further developed in constant embodiment of their quality.

The ritualized basic exercises on the four animals make it easier for patients to familiarize themselves with the new patterns of movement that have been developed for them and thus gain confidence. They are reduced to essentials in their range of motion. This enables the trained diagnostic eye to clearly identify the development potential to be aimed at in order to promote the required perception and expression skills.

Especially the areas of perception and expression are severely blocked and damaged, especially in the case of patients who are additionally post-traumatically burdened.

Your own point of view and place indisputably fixed as to claim a bear, to be proud and glorious like a crane and to use the space offered, to raise your hands and claws to defend yourself against border violations or to create a suitably pleasurable coexistence like the snake in a wise manner is often impossible for these patients at the beginning of the treatment.

Good physicality, a committed invitation and, above all, the promotion of 'giving permission' for new experiences are co-determining prerequisites for recovery. Many patients acquire 'inner helpers' who promote security and encourage others to do so, which they learn to use in a targeted way in a common, biographical and context-related therapeutic discussion.

It is not uncommon for bears, cranes, tigers and snakes to be found in the emergency case as a picture or in the form of photos, in which the tools to cope with frightening situations are collected.

The above mentioned is only an incomplete selection of important aspects, which come into play through the inclusion of the Qigong Dancing elements in my work with (traumatized) addicted people.

The overall aim of body therapy is to change inveterate information stored in neuronal networked structures. It is precisely these new connections that are necessary for healing can be achieved in a special way by including all levels of experience from motor activity, cognition, emotion, volition, affectivity and spirituality, as is aimed for in Gertrud's Qigong Dancing.

'Use it or lose it' also means that careful practice is undoubtedly necessary.

UTE BUSSE
SCHOOL EXPERIENCES

For a year I worked with the pupils at the school 'Schule am Weser-bogen' in Bad Oeynhausen in 2015/16. It is a at a fostering school focussing on physical and motoric developement.

Silvestro Leanza, a young boy told us about his understanding of the relationship between the dragon and the four animals:

The dragon carries four animals in him.

The first animal is the bear:
The bear and the dragon are very similar, because both are living in a cave

The second animal is the crane:
The dragon and the crane have the same energy. They use this energy to fly.

The third animal is the tiger:
The dragon and the tiger are very dangerous and strong, because they have the same claws. Both of them never give up.

The fourth animal is the snake:
The dragon and the snake are very long and flexible. They can both wrap their prey around.

Der Drache hat vier Tiere in sich

Das erste Tier ist der Bär.
Der Bär und der Drache sind sich sehr ähnlich,
weil beide in einer Höhle wohnen.

Das zweite Tier ist der Kranich.
Der Drache und der Kranich haben die
selbe Kraft. Die Kraft nutzen sie zum Fliegen.

Das dritte Tier ist der Tiger.
Der Drache und der Tiger sind sehr gefährlich
und stark, denn beide geben nie auf -
weil der Tiger und der Drache
die selben Krallen haben.

Das vierte Tier ist die Schlange.
Der Drache und die Schlange sind beide sehr lang
und gelenkig und können
beide ihre Beute umwickeln.

Silvestro Leanza

154

ACKNOWLEDGMENT

My journey of writing a book continued with my desicion to translate it in English. It was an adventure to carefully examine every message. The four animals have been with me again. The bear reminded me of my fundamental knowledge and experience I have gained over the years – that is my basis. The crane supported me in my vision to bring the energy of the four animals into the world and reach every interested person. The tiger gave me the drive to move on because I believe in the essential practising and keeping it alive, even though there are so many 'easy going' offers on the market. With the sensual aspect of the snake I enjoyed the further developement of my work.

Thanks to the support of some friends. Translating my book became a beautiful experience for the next step that I am very excited about, because my work only stays alive only when people work with it and develop it further.

I want to mention some good friends. The first critical voice was Jörg Kruse, who helped me to translate step by step and to reconsider each expression. Kerstin Donaldson with her husband Fred had a look at some special paragraphs. My old student Birgit came back on the scene just in the right moment to make some fine adjustments. We had a lot of fun together. A big surprise was Stephanie Michaelis, also an old student of mine. Her knowledge of the English language made her a good corrector. And very great thanks to Alex Viehmann, Carola Benz and Birgitta Wolf. They had a supportive look for eliminating mistakes. The native spreaker Keith Glascock gave a good support with his excellent understanding to find the right words for special expressions. I appreciate a lot his support. Everyone has invested time to support this project, so I ask all readers in the English-speaking countries to bear in mind, that this translation was not done by a native speaker, but with the heart to bring the energy of the four animals into the world.

The photos are from Gert Eichberger, Jo Fahl, Thomas Hansmann, Wilhelm Junker and Jana Wippermann. The paintings are from Kerstin Michels, Silvestro Lanza, Ralf Assmann and Josiane Baudart. It is always a joy to look at the powerful expressions.

Thank you for the valuable contributions and reports from Ute Busse, Patrick Frottier, Wolfgang Gratz, Mario Mayr, Philipp Pümpel, Thomas Rinner, Thomas from Vienna, Carsten Schubert and Christoph Schwarz.

Thanks to Milan Müller, who did the QR-codes from the exercises. And of course the clips themselves – well, Andreas Lindlar the filmmaker, my husband Steve Schroyder and Holger Teuber the musicians. I feel honored by their work.

And Pepe Pazzerello for his creative input, graphic stuff and the layout of the book. Thanks for that.

During the process of putting my work into words I finally realized:

If you really wish to understand my book please feel welcome to join my teaching.

MUSIC - DVD - BOOK

MUSIC:

MIT DEN VIER TIEREN BEWEGEN
Christoph Schwarz, Wien 2014

QIGONG DANCING
Steve Schroyder & AlienVoices
2012 OXOZmusic, Irina Sheba Music

DVD:

QIGONG DANCING – DER TANZ MIT DER LEBENSENERGIE
WARNER VISION, 2000

ANGEWANDTES QIGONG - LONG PING
EIGENVERTRIEB, 2017

• DVD 1: QIGONG DANCING
Exercises to join

• DVD 2: TAIJI | QIGONG | KUNG FU
Exercises from the Dojo Friedlicher Drache

All articles are available at Planetware Onlineshop:
www.planetware.de

BOOKS:

KRAFT DER VIER TIERE
Gertrud Schröder - Long Ping

ENERGY OF THE FOUR ANIMALS
Gertrud Schröder - Long Ping

WEBSITES:

www.friedlicherdrache.de
www.affektkontrolltraining.de
www.animotion.life
www.geistigeselbstverteidigung.de
www.wolfgang-gratz.at
www.moment.co.at
www.schroyder.de
www.alienvoices.de
www.pepworx.de